they are my forebears

karen foster
design

Ancestry Art

Create unforgettable ancestry scrapbooks, theme books, boxes and more using vintage photos, stories and documents.

Dedication

This book is dedicated to my grandmother, Mary Porter, who taught me through her example to cherish my ancestors.

their legacy
lives on in me

Contents

I am who I am because of the sacrifices they made

AUTHOR · Karen Foster
EDITOR · Caroll Shreeve COPY EDITOR · Amy Lynn Smith
ART DIRECTOR · Jennifer Straus
DESIGNER · Glenda Smith
GENEALOGY CONSULTANT · D. Joshua Taylor

Published by
Karen Foster Design
623 North 1250 West
Centerville, Utah 84014

ISBN 0-9753703-051699

Ask for Karen Foster scrapbook products at your favorite scrapbook store.
To locate a store selling Karen Foster products, visit www.karenfosterdesign.com. Click on Retail Store Directory. If the products are unavailable in your area, order online at www.scrapbookpaper.com.

Printed in the United States of America

KAREN FOSTER
· D E S I G N ·

Grandma's Search for *Mary*

As I began the search for my ancestors, I sometimes felt they were sitting beside me. I found myself imagining what they were like, and I wanted to meet them. The search took me on an unexpected but wonderful journey.

Remembering...

For as long as I can remember, my grandmother, Mary Porter, took an hour-long bus ride every Wednesday to the Family History Library in Salt Lake City, Utah. She searched for ancestors and filled her dining-room filing cabinet with endless genealogy records, pedigree charts, life stories and family group sheets. For Christmas she gave her grandchildren family history books containing copies of these records. I would have preferred toys.

Karen's grandmother, Mary Porter, as a young lady.

The summer after my high school graduation, I decided to meet Grandma at the library to help her. She taught me how to locate microfilmed records containing christenings, marriages, burials, wills and census records. She told me the names I was to look for in each film.

Researching with Grandma

It was tedious work for a teenager. Sometimes the writing was difficult to read. Often I felt tired and bored. But it was worth it if we found one name allowing us to fill in a blank.

Heaven sent

There is a spirit in family history research that brings a connection to ancestors attainable in no other way.

MARRIAGES solemn
in the County of

I love you grandma Mary

Grandma Mary Roe was born to goodly parents who tried to teach the right ways of life on February 16, 1900 in the little town of Escalante, Utah. Her childhood was during the horse and buggy days. Her first time out of Escalante was to go to Marysvale in a horse-drawn wagon with her family. the wagon was filled with fruit to sell and they brought back supplies for the winter.

Heaven sent

Sometimes I felt like a detective. If parents were not born in the same town as their children, we tried to find them in the records of neighboring towns. Consulting maps, we searched in a radius around the town spiraling outward. If people had never moved away from their hometowns, it would have made our search easier. Grandma was thrilled with my discovery of a baby girl that she had missed. Two daughters of a family had been given the same name; the second being named for her deceased sister—a common practice at that time. While I was pleased to have made a difference, at the time I couldn't understand her joy.

Four Mary Hacketts
Grandma often talked about her great-grandmother, Mary Hackett. She had a record of Mary's 1807 marriage in Radford, Nottinghamshire, England, but connecting Mary to parents had remained an elusive task for decades. There were four Mary

Hacketts born around the same time. Figuring out which one was ours had stumped Grandma as well as her mother before her. "When I get to heaven," Grandma often said, "I'm going ask Mary Hackett which one she was, and if I can figure out how to tell you I will."

When summer came to an end, I left for college and didn't go to the library with Grandma anymore. After a few years she couldn't go there anymore, either. She often said, "I'd die happy if I knew someone would take my genealogy records." My mother volunteered. Grandma died a few years later.

Starting Again

Recently, I began going to the library with my mother, who had continued the search for Mary Hackett. Though the card catalog had been replaced by a computer, I was able to locate films needed to continue the search. The pedigree charts and life histories Grandma had given me as a child took on new meaning. I studied each of the four Mary Hacketts and asked endless questions of librarians and professional genealogists. "How do I know which Mary Hackett is the right one?" Choosing the wrong one would start me on a path following the wrong family line. One professional genealogist said, "You have to follow your best hunch and see where it leads." I focused on the Mary born in 1767 to Thomas and Catherine Hackett in Bulwell. In these records, I found the births of many of her siblings and the death of her mother, but I could not find the death of her father. This missing clue would become important to my search.

Following a Hunch

I tried to tie her to our Mary that I knew was married in Radford. Following the advice of one librarian, I looked up Thomas' will to see if he had named Mary and her husband as beneficiaries; there was nothing. I became discouraged. Finally, one librarian said, "Look for Thomas Hackett's death in the town where Mary was married. Maybe he went to stay with her as an old man."

It was a long shot. I searched the Radford film without much hope. I was sleepy that day and dozing at the microfilm machine. I turned the crank, dozed, and sleepily read endless names. There were no Hacketts in Radford. I dozed again. Suddenly, my eyes blinked open, and there it was, "Burial, Thomas Hackett, February 7, 1802"! A picture came into my mind of Thomas as an old man being cared for in a neighboring town by his daughter until he died. I like to think that Grandma nudged me awake, just at the right moment.

Passing It On

I recently took my daughter to the library. I taught her how to find the microfilm and look for names. She found Mary's grandparents and great-grandparents. I was overjoyed when she found a child we almost missed. Now she's gone to college and doesn't have time to help, but when the time is right for her, she'll know what to do.

The only records I have of the life of Mary Hackett are of her christening, marriage and burial, and a census record proclaiming her a lace maker. I wish I knew more about her. But I will remember her, and I want my children to remember her. The search brought me feelings of love for my forebears that I had never known before.

Honoring My Ancestors

This experience gave me the desire to create this book and a line of ancestry scrapbook papers and stickers. It is my hope that something will stir within you a desire to search out and become acquainted with your ancestors. The information you find and preserve can become a precious family heirloom for generations to come.

Karen Foster

These ancestry papers can help you organize your family history.

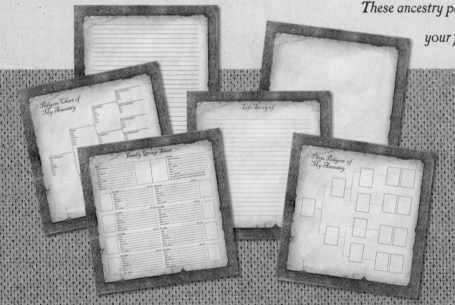

I Love You, Grandma Mary
(opposite page)
by Jennifer Straus

Supplies
Paper: Immigrant Collage, Black Letter, Shabby Brown by KFD
Stickers: Old Tags, Remember, Old Alphabet by KFD
Fiber: unknown
Paper Clip

To create a scrapbook treasure for your family, write life stories about parents, grandparents and great-grandparents. Learning about their lives and the challenges they faced will endear them to you.

Hunsaker Story
by Caroll Shreeve

Supplies
Paper: Life Story, Life Story Continued, Red Crackle, Antique Lace, Shabby Dark by KFD
Stickers: Old Tags by KFD
Fabric: unknown
Embellishments: Karen Foster Metals by KFD
Metallic Rub Ons: by Craf-T Products

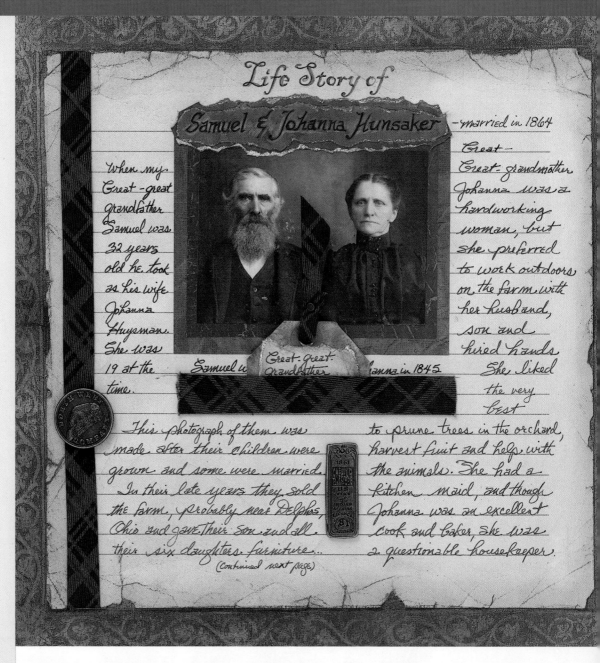

Life Story of

Samuel & Johanna Hunsaker — married in 1864

When my Great-great grandfather Samuel was 32 years old he took as his wife Johanna Huysman. She was 19 at the time.

Great-Great-grandmother Johanna was a hardworking woman, but she preferred to work outdoors on the farm with her husband, son and hired hands. She liked the very best

Samuel w... Great-great-grandfather ...anna in 1845

This photograph of them was made after their children were grown and some were married. In their late years they sold the farm, probably near Delphos, Ohio and gave their son and all their six daughters furniture...
(Continued next page)

to prune trees in the orchard, harvest fruit and help with the animals. She had a kitchen maid, and though Johanna was an excellent cook and baker, she was a questionable housekeeper.

Caroll wrote the story of her grandparents in her own handwriting. It gives a touch of warmth to the project and her descendents will appreciate her for it.

Life Stories

Instructions

Begin with your own story. Collect documents such as birth, death, marriage, and graduation certificates. Also search diaries, letters, report cards, awards, and photos (especially those with names and dates). You will later use these elements to illustrate your life stories.

Put these items in a box and set it where you will see it every day. Add documents to the box for several weeks. Ask relatives for more information and write what you discover on 3" x 5" cards. Add these to the box. These items will help you write a timeline followed by the life story.

Lay out all the items chronologically in three groups: childhood, teen years, and adulthood. Looking at the documentation will help you write up a timeline and begin a rough draft. You may want to start like this:

"I was born in _____ on _____. My parents' names are _____. I was the _____ child of _____ children. The names of my siblings are _____ ..." and so on.

Referring to the documents and following the timeline, write or type the story. When it is refined, write or type the story on the Life Story and Life Story Continued papers.

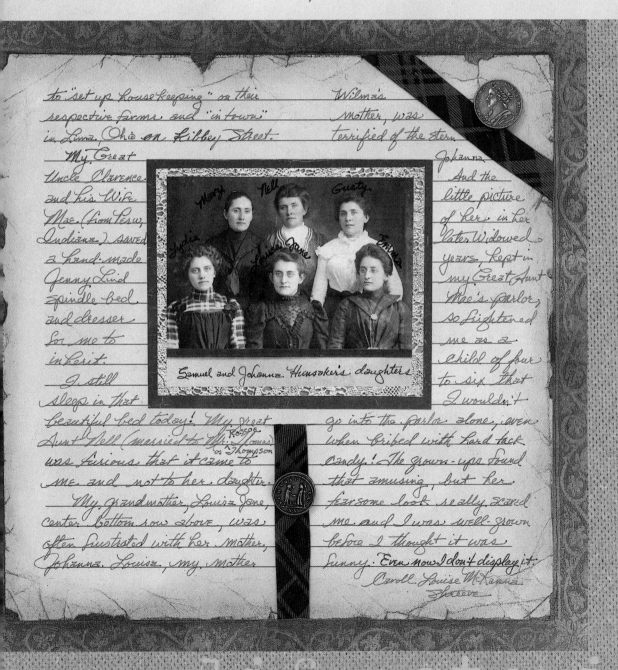

to "set up housekeeping" on their respective farms and "in town" in Lima, Ohio on Kibbey Street.

My Great Uncle Clarence and his Wife Mae (from Peru, Indiana) saved a hand-made Jenny Lind spindle bed and dresser for me to inherit.

I still sleep in that beautiful bed today! My great Aunt Nell (married to Mr. Rosspe Thomas or Thompson) was furious that it came to me and not to her daughter.

My grandmother, Louisa Jane, center bottom row above, was often frustrated with her mother, Johanna. Louisa, my mother

Wilma's mother, was terrified of the stern Johanna. And the little picture of her in her later widowed years, kept in my Great Aunt Mae's parlor, so frightened me as a child of four to six that I wouldn't go into the parlor alone, even when bribed with hard tack candy! The grown-ups found that amusing, but her fearsome look really scared me and I was well-grown before I thought it was funny. Even now I don't display it.

Carroll Louise McKanna Shreeve

Caption on photo: Mary · Nell · Gusty · Lydia · Louisa Jane · Emma
Samuel and Johanna Hunsaker's daughters

life stories

A handwritten story will mean more to your descendents, but the papers can fit into some old electric typewriters for typing. You may want to illustrate the layout with several photos.

Repeat this process for each story you write. Keep them short and simple, focusing on one story at a time so the task doesn't become daunting. You don't need to include every detail, and the stories don't require perfection. You can make changes or add details later.

As you gather documents about your parents and grandparents, interview them using a video camera or tape recorder. Ask questions that will stimulate memories and feelings.

Record new dates and places of births, marriages and deaths as you discover them in your search. Include the information on pedigree charts and family group sheets. Make copies of the photos and documents in the possession of other relatives. These may

provide additional information and become part of your ancestry art.

Encourage your children to write their own life stories. Help them remember important events and stimulate their writing by asking them what they like to do and how they think and feel about things. Very young children can dictate their stories to you. As years pass, growing and changing children can update their stories with new experiences, photos and achievements.

To make a hidden pocket where tags containing information can be stored, cut a slit in the paper. Attach a rectangle of paper to the back of the layout to act as the pocket. Decorate the opening with lace or trim.

REMEMBER

Life Story of
Mary Roe and Leland Porter

Through my teenage years, my life was full of fun, having dancing and skating. One night at a dance, my brother, Wilford, danced with me and told me that Lee was going to ask me for a date that night. Boy! Was I scared! Lee was quite the popular person, good looking and all of that. Well, I didn't know what to do, so I asked Wilford what should I say. "Make an excuse if you don't want to go", he told me. So When Ellis Mitchell danced with me and ask me for a date, I gladly accepted. When Lee asked if he could take me home I said, "I'd rather be excused."

But I was determined to go with him, so the next time I got the chance, I took it. The more I went with him, the more I liked him. Soon we were going steady. Lee received his call to go into the Army in the First World War and he asked me to marry him before he left. I was 18 at the time and very much in love with him. We were married in Escalante, Utah, on the 17th of May 1918, so we were married only two months before he had to leave on July 24.

Lee returned home in February 1919 from the war. Oh, Happy Day! Our town was so scared of getting the flu again that every soldier was quarantined for a week before folks felt safe around them. I quit my job so that I could be quarantined with Lee. The bottom had dropped out of everything so few jobs were to be had. A little sheep-herding was all there was for men in Escalante. The sheep men would let the boys take turns herding the sheep for them. So when it was Lee's turn, I went with him for our honeymoon.

friends brave

Life Story of Mary Roe Porter
by Jennifer Straus

Supplies
Paper: Life Story by KFD
Stickers: Remember by KFD
Military Tag: Family heirloom

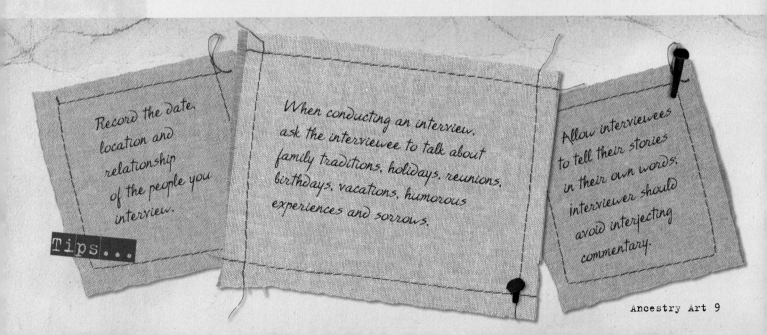

Record the date, location and relationship of the people you interview.

When conducting an interview, ask the interviewee to talk about family traditions, holidays, reunions, birthdays, vacations, humorous experiences and sorrows.

Allow interviewees to tell their stories in their own words; interviewer should avoid interjecting commentary.

Tips...

Saddle Up My Susie
by Caroll Shreeve

Caroll "Susie" McKanna

In the summer of 1947, before I was
five, a photographer brought his paint
Lima, Ohio. I
pony to ... "real"
...

In 1957 mom gave ma
my first oil pa...

Western ...!

Saddle Up My Susie
by Caroll Shreeve

Supplies

Paper: Stitched Leather, Pieced Leather, Old Script, Parish Records, Life Story Continued by KFD
Brown Vellum: unknown
Stickers: Saddle Up, Old Alphabet by KFD
Chestnut and Light Blue Mini Brads: by KFD

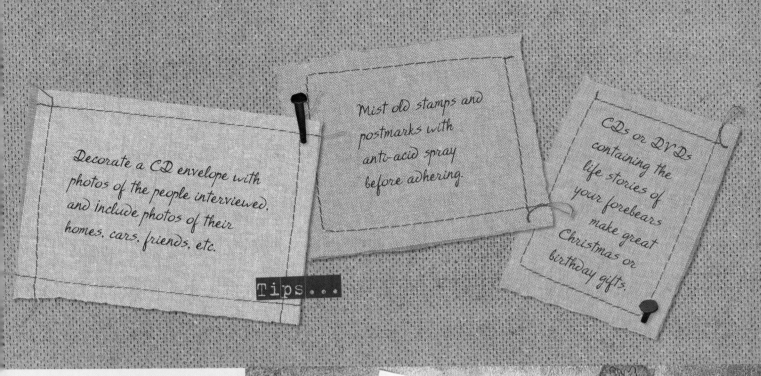

Decorate a CD envelope with photos of the people interviewed. and include photos of their homes. cars. friends. etc.

Tips...

Mist old stamps and postmarks with anti-acid spray before adhering.

CDs or DVDs containing the life stories of your forebears make great Christmas or birthday gifts.

CD Holder
by Joy Candrian

Supplies
Paper: Shabby Dark, Parchment Border by KFD
Buttons and Fibers: unknown

life stories

Digitally capture your interviews of parents, grandparents and other relatives.

Burn the images on a CD or DVD. Create an artistic envelope to hold the disk.

Adhere it to a scrapbook page.

- 9/6/1885 birth record
- 1886 christening Methodist church record
- 1902 photo high school graduation
- 1902 diploma
- 1919 Train trip to St. Louis photo w/cigar
- 1919 in bow tie & Prince Albert great coat/day he bought the first of three farms./photo
- 1943 photo family group shot w/wife Mae/marriage date unknown.
- 1966-death Memorial Service program
- grave marker in Columbus Grove, Ohio photo

Clarence W. Hunsaker 1885-1966 Ohio

Memorial Service

Cuff link from his only silk shirt.

HUNSAKER

Along with your ancestor's timeline, scrapbook reduced copies of old documents such as funeral programs and certificates.

Tip...

Hunsaker Timeline
by Caroll Shreeve

Supplies
Paper: Map Collage, Shadow Box, Deep Green Crackle, Cinnamon Stick, Dusty Rose Crackle, Parched Leather, Shabby Parchment by KFD
Crystal Lacquer: by Sakura Hobby Craft
Fibers: by Making Memories; Darice
Alphabet Stickers: by Sticko Inspirables
Clasp: Karen Foster Metals by KFD
Antique Mini Brads: by KFD
Metal Button: Caroll's father's

Timeline Baby
by Caroll Shreeve

Supplies
Paper: Shabby Map, Parish Records, Antique Parchment, Parched Leather, Old Scroll by KFD
Stickers: Timeless Treasures by NRN Designs
Copper Paint: Top Color Enamel by Pelikan
Crystal Lacquer: by Sakura Hobby Craft
Antique Mini Brads: by KFD

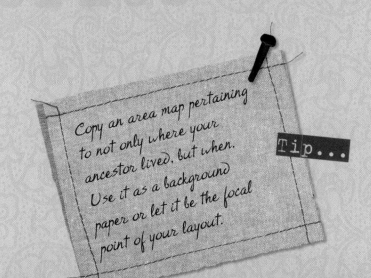

Copy an area map pertaining to not only where your ancestor lived, but when. Use it as a background paper or let it be the focal point of your layout.

Tip...

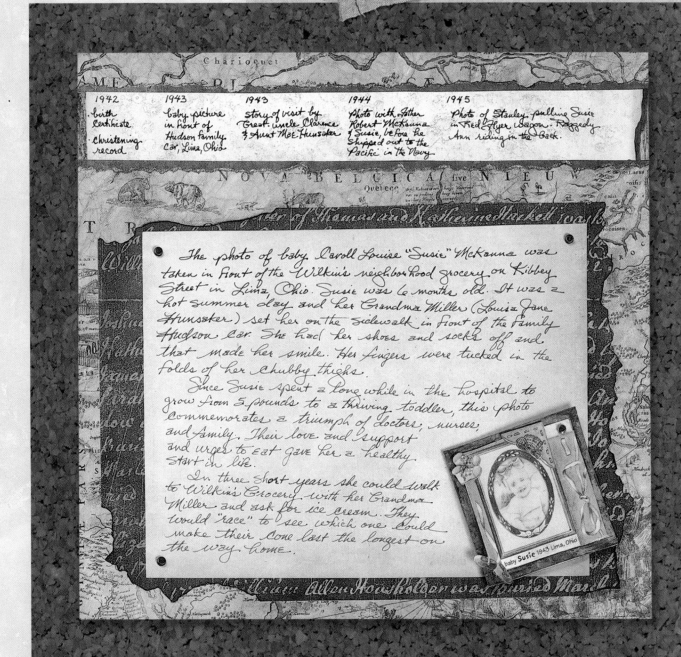

1942
birth certificate
christening record

1943
baby picture in front of Hudson family car, Lima, Ohio

1943
Story of visit by Great-uncle Clarence & Aunt Mae Hunsaker

1944
Photo with Father Robert McKenna & Susie, before he Shipped out to the Pacific in the Navy

1945
Photo of Stanley pulling Susie in Red Flyer Wagon. Raggedy Ann riding in the Back.

The photo of baby Caroll Louise "Susie" McKenna was taken in front of the Wilkin's neighborhood grocery on Kibbey Street in Lima, Ohio. Susie was 6 months old. It was a hot summer day and her Grandma Miller (Louisa Jane Hunsaker) set her on the sidewalk in front of the family Hudson car. She had her shoes and socks off and that made her smile. Her fingers were tucked in the folds of her chubby thighs.

Since Susie spent a long while in the hospital to grow from 5 pounds to a thriving toddler, this photo commemorates a triumph of doctors, nurses, and family. Their love and support and urges to eat gave her a healthy start in life.

In three short years she could walk to Wilkin's Grocery with her Grandma Miller and ask for ice cream. They would "race" to see which one could make their cone last the longest on the way home.

baby Susie 1943 Lima, Ohio

Chapter 2

Pedigree Charts

A pedigree chart is a diagram of your family tree tracing your ancestry back through the generations.

Family Tree
by Debra Wilcox

Supplies
Paper: Pedigree Chart, Shabby Map, Old Family Tree by KFD
Stickers: Old Tags, Remember by KFD

Instructions

To fill out a Pedigree Chart, start with yourself as the son or daughter and work backward. Fill in as much information as you can regarding names, dates and places pertaining to parents, grandparents and great-grandparents. Be consistent in how you write information. Write all four digits in the year and use the correct genealogical standards: Places in the U.S.: Town, County, State. Other Countries: Parish or Town, County or Province, Country.

Ask family members for more information. Search for old journals, letters, certificates, immigration papers, passports and family Bibles. You may also find information in church, probate, property and census records. Other helpful sources are cemeteries, family history libraries and Internet sites (see inside back cover). Make copies of all your documents for safekeeping. Create a research log of where you have searched and of documents you store. When asked to lend documents to others, keep a list of documents and where they went.

If you trace lines back further than the spaces allow, start new Pedigree Charts with great-grandparents as sons or daughters. Number their names and list corresponding numbers on new charts.

Debra used calligraphy to create this beautiful pedigree chart of her husband's lineage.

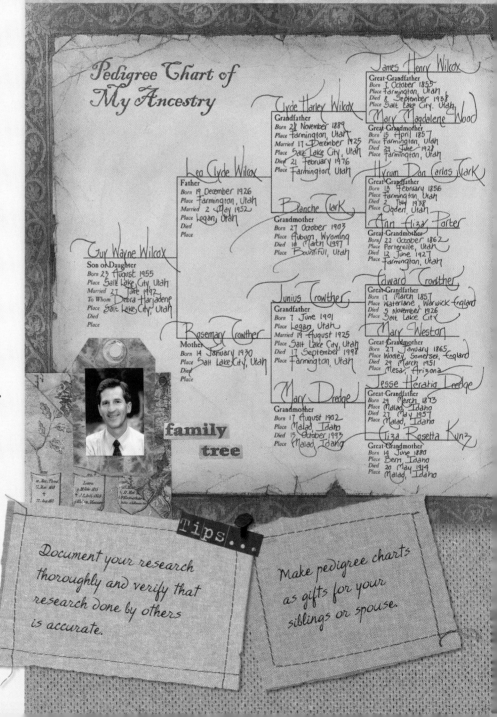

Tips....

Document your research thoroughly and verify that research done by others is accurate.

Make pedigree charts as gifts for your siblings or spouse.

Photo Pedigree

Have you ever wondered where your father's strong jaw or your grandmother's beautiful eyes came from? The Photo Pedigree Chart can help family members trace facial features to previous generations. This collection of ancestry photos will become an heirloom for posterity.

Instructions

To complete a Photo Pedigree Chart, adhere a photo of yourself in the space on the left. In the additional spaces provided, adhere photos of your parents, grandparents, and so on. Ask relatives for copies of photos. Make extra copies for other family members. Photos do not need to fit in the rectangles; they are provided as a guide. Near each photo, write your ancestor's name, if desired, or position the Photo Pedigree Chart directly opposite the Pedigree Chart in your scrapbook binder.

If you can find more photos or paintings of ancestors than the spaces on this sheet allow, start new Photo Pedigree Charts with the photos of your great-grandparents in the spaces on the left. Use the numbering system described on the previous page.

If some photos are unavailable, fill the space with a matching mat on which the person's name is written.

Photo Pedigree
by Debra Wilcox

Supplies
Paper: Photo Pedigree Chart, Shabby Map, Old Family Tree by KFD
Stickers: Ancestry Definitions, Old Tags, Old Documents by KFD

Tip...

Use a light table to write out the pedigree information on a sheet of lightweight paper laid over the top of the Pedigree Chart. When certain you have written it correctly, switch places with the Pedigree Chart and the overlay and trace the words onto the Pedigree Chart.

Debra matted photographs of the couples with matching shapes to help identify the pairs and add to the interest of the page.

8 **eight** GENEr

Me,
Julia Burgon
June, 29 1983

My photograph
was taken in
August of 2000,
the summer before
my senior year at
San Lorenzo Valley
High School.
My senior year
turned out to be
a great success and
I kept myself
busy with
student government,
cheerleading,
yearbook
and diving.

My Mother,
Andrea Sharp
May 9, 1954

Her photograph
was taken in 1976,
the year she
graduated from
Brigham
Young University
in graphic design.
She taught me about
the masters of art
throughout my life
by volunteering in
my grade school
classrooms.
She has set a
wonderful example
to me as a mother.

My Grandmother,
Edith Porter
November 3, 1919

Her photograph
was taken in 1950,
just after she married
a city boy,
my grandfather,
Richard Sharp.
The corsage she
is wearing is
from her husband.
My grandmother
has always been
an example to me
and I hope to follow
her footsteps and
one day work
in the temple
with my husband.

My Great
Grandfather,
Leland Porter
August 9, 1894

His photograph
was taken in 1910,
when he was
16 years old.
When he grew up
he owned a saw mill
in a small town in
Southern Utah.
My grandmother
remembers him
sometimes giving
out lumber free
of charge. He
loved life and
was always kind
to everyone.

8 Generations
by Julia Burgon

Supplies
White Vellum: Visions
Paper: Dusty Rose Crackle, Soft Green
Crackle, White Crackle, Yellow Crackle,
Shabby Dark, Erased Chalkboard by KFD
Stickers: Alphabet Tags by KFD
Ribbon: by Darice
White Mini Brads: by KFD

Julia's mother, Andrea, made 2" x 3" copies of the
above eight generations of portraits. Together,
Andrea and Julia researched and wrote the captions
for each portrait. Julia then created this two-page
layout using the photos and research.

Eight Generations

My Great, Great,
Grandmother,
Alice Lovina Griffin
March 21, 1856

Alice was one of
5 out of 10 children
that lived to adulthood.
She was a small,
gentle lady
whose children
and grandchildren
adored her.
My grandma
remembers
asking her for
a piece of
bread and butter.
She responded,
"I don't have any butter,
but I would love to
give you some
cream and sugar."

My Great, Great,
Great Grandmother,
Sarah Smith
October 2, 1837

Her photograph
was taken when she
was a young mother
with only two children.
Her mother,
Jerusha Barden,
died eleven days
after giving
birth to her.
Her father,
Hyrum Smith,
was murdered
when she was only
seven years old.
She walked across
the plains when
she was eleven.

My Great, Great,
Great, Great
Grandfather,
Hyrum Smith
February 9, 1800

His portrait
was painted by
G. and R.L. Corbett.
Hyrum was a man
dedicated to the Lord
and His service.
He stood by His brother,
Joseph Smith,
as he endured
persecutions of all kinds.
Hyrum was taken to
Carthage Jail
with Joseph where
they were both
murdered by
an outraged mob.

My Great, Great,
Great, Great, Great,
Grandmother,
Lucy Mack
July 8, 1775

As a young mother,
Lucy nearly died
from consumption.
As the night wore on she
was expected to die.
She promised the Lord
that if He let her live,
she would dedicate
her life to serving Him.
Her friends and
family were overjoyed
to see her recover
the next morning.
Lucy fulfilled her promise
by rearing a son who
became a prophet of God.

For your wall, frame
a group of generational
portraits in a specially
cut mat with several
windows.

When children become
involved in creating ancestry
scrapbooks, they are more
likely to become interested
in carrying on the research.

Generational
layouts can depict
as little as three
or four generations
or more than the
eight shown above.

Tips...

While pedigree charts help you document the marriage relationships in your lineage, family group sheets help you document the relationships between spouses, parents and children.

Family Group Sheets

Instructions

1. Start by creating a Family Group Sheet of your own family, listing yourself as a parent (if applicable). Fill out another sheet with yourself as a child. Create sheets for each of your parents as children, and for each couple listed on your Pedigree Chart. Although there are spaces for photos, you can document vital family information even if photos are not available.

2. Record the children of each family in order of their births and include all members of the family unit whether they are living or not. If there are more than eight children in the family, list additional children on another Family Group Sheet being sure to list the parents a second time.

3. Create Family Group Sheets for couples with no children and for unmarried couples or divorced couples who had children together.

4. If a parent remarried, create a separate Family Group Sheet for that couple and any children from that union.

5. Record the complete maiden name of each female. If it is not available, list her married name.

6. As you work back in time, you may want to use a numbering system to keep your information organized. Number each couple on the Pedigree Chart as described on page 14, with corresponding numbers on the Family Group Sheets. For example, put a number by your paternal great-grandparents on your Pedigree Chart and write a corresponding number by their names on the Family Group Sheet. This will help you track them easily.

7. Organize your scrapbook with the Pedigree Chart first, followed by the associated Family Group Sheets. Intersperse them with artful layouts containing life stories, photos, documents, and memorabilia. Make sure the information you document is consistent and accurate.

Software programs are available to organize family groups and pedigree charts. See inside back cover.

Help your children make their own copy of the family group sheet listing themselves as children.

On the back of your sheets, and in a separate log, document your sources to prevent duplicating your search.

Tips...

Primary and Secondary Sources

If an ancestor's vital information was written at the time it occurred by someone present, it is called a primary source. If it was written afterward by someone who was not present, it is called a secondary source. Although secondary sources are helpful, they are sometimes inaccurate. For example, a birth certificate is a primary source, but a census record is a secondary source. A parish register is a primary source of christenings, marriages and burials, whereas a bishop's transcript is a copy of the register and, as a secondary source, may contain errors.

Family Group Sheet
by Karen Foster

Supplies
Paper: Family Group Sheet by KFD

Research Tips

Make sure your family relationships are firmly connected and documented. A mistake could send you down the wrong family line. Here are some tips to help you avoid confusion and solve problems.

A family name no longer found in the town
If you believe the family moved away, try searching records of other towns in an outward spiral around the original town. If you find nothing, try searching migration and immigration records.

A variety of spellings for the same surname
Various name spellings may all represent the people you are looking for. Spelling was inconsistent and not considered important.

People with identical names
Search for clues that tie them to dates, locations and the people you are trying to connect them to. For example, a father may name his children and their spouses in his will or a census may give names and dates that match up.

Tracking a newly married couple
In some places a girl married in her hometown then moved to the town where her husband worked. Often she returned home for the birth of her first baby.

A name change at the point of immigration
Look for similar names with the spelling shortened, altered or simplified.

Too many years between babies
Babies were usually born every couple of years. If you notice a bigger time span, you may have missed a birth or the mother may have died.

Two babies with the same name
Babies were sometimes named for deceased siblings.

Inaccurate census records
Although census records are helpful, census-takers sometimes recorded inaccurate information.

Scrapbooking Your Research

As you research information about your ancestors, you will collect a variety of documents and photos along the way. This chapter will give you ideas to scrapbook your findings.

The largest pocket holds Fredrich Paul's will in German and English. Smaller pockets contain text from his tombstone and the grave registration record. In the journaling box beneath the title, Joy describes the things she has learned about this ancestor.

Photoless Scrapbook Pages

When we think of scrapbooks, we think of photographs. However, the documents you discover about some ancestors may be your only record. Make scrapbook layouts using these documents as the focal point of each layout. This art, along with other ancestry layouts you create, will make a beautiful ancestry scrapbook.

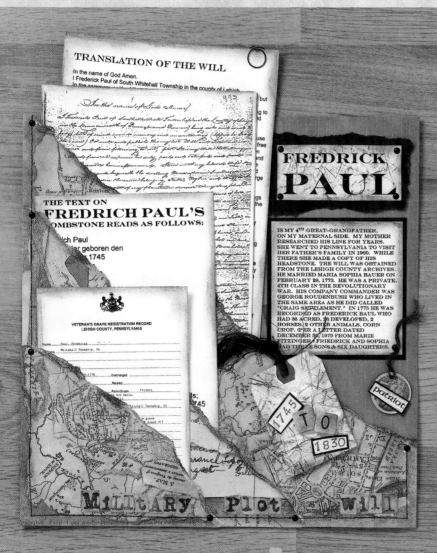

Fredrich Paul
by Joy Candrian

Supplies
Papers: Map Collage, Immigrant Collage, Gold Stitched, Shabby Map, Shabby Parchment by KFD
Stickers: Old Alphabet, Old Tags by KFD
Black Mini Brads: by KFD
Tag: by Making Memories
Fibers: unknown

Joy described her search for information about this ancestor on the tags in the small lower pockets. The documents themselves are tucked into the large upper pocket.

Maria Magdelina Dick

by Joy Candrian

Supplies

Paper: Wanted Poster, Old Book Cover, Antique Parchment, Parchment Border, Dusty Yellow Crackle by KFD
Mini Tags: by Stampin' Up!
Metallic Rub Ons: by Craf-T Products
Beige and Brown Cardstock: by Bazzill Basics

Instructions

1. Stamp image onto Dusty Yellow Crackle paper.

2. Cover stamped images with copper embossing powder, shake off excess. Heat-set images.

3. Add torn-edged borders rubbed with copper metallics to all pockets.

4. Add ancestor's name-paper to center pocket. Rub torn edges with metallics.

5. Computer-generate information about relationship to ancestor, print, tear edges, rub with metallics, adhere to large pocket.

6. With brown thread, sew pockets onto the page. Add vintage button.

7. Chalk mini-tag information.

8. Print ancestor's life story onto beige cardstock, cut out unevenly. Outline with black marker. Adhere to large tags cut from cardstock.

9. Copy all documents onto beige cardstock, tuck into large pocket.

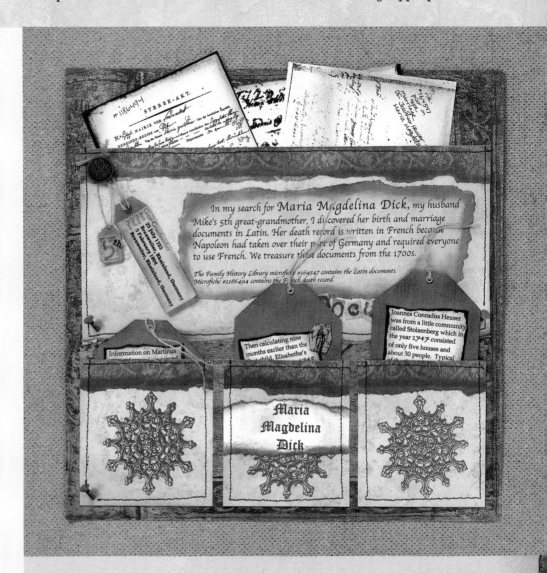

Create a Working Binder

If you are serious about genealogical research, make photocopies of documents and organize them in an undecorated binder you can take with you to family history libraries, cemeteries and other places of research. Using family history computer software (see inside back cover), digitally organize your family group sheets and pedigree charts. Your working binder should include these sheets, copies of pertinent documents and a research log.

Make copies of all your documents and store for safekeeping. Make extra copies to use in your ancestry scrapbook.

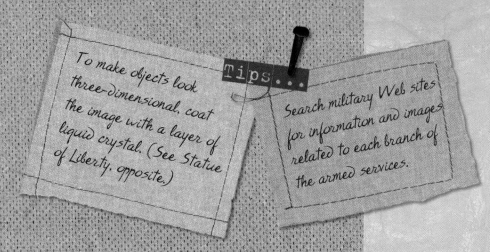

Tips...

To make objects look three-dimensional, coat the image with a layer of liquid crystal. (See Statue of Liberty, opposite.)

Search military Web sites for information and images related to each branch of the armed services.

I will remember

my heritage

Add age and distress to quotes and games by crumpling, chalking or sponging with walnut dye. Use Bingo Cards and Domino Cut Outs to offset old black-and-white photos.

Bingo Shadow Box
by Karen Foster

Supplies
Paper: Shadow Box by KFD
Quotes: Heritage Cut & Tear Quotes by KFD
Cut & Tear Games: Bingo Cards & Domino Cut Outs by KFD
Stickers: Old Ticket Stubs by KFD
Buckle, Buttons, Key and Postage Stamps: Karen's family heirlooms

memorabilia

Navy Brothers
by Caroll Shreeve

Supplies
Papers: Antique Parchment, Patriotic Collage, Red Crackle, Blue Crackle, Dusty Yellow Crackle, Shell Border, Cinnamon Swirl by KFD
Stickers: Military and Freedom by KFD
Rubber Stamps: by Hero Arts
Navy Blue and White Mini Brads: by KFD
Crystal Lacquer: by Sakura Hobby Craft

Caroll rubber-stamped the title and colored it with colored pencils. She tucked photos and documents of her father's Navy experiences into the vertical pocket. She also attached his Navy pins to the layout.

New Hampshire Farmhouse Ladies
by Anita Crane

Supplies
Papers: Parish Records, Purple Stitched, Winter Words Blue, Map Collage, Old Book Liner by KFD
Stickers: Old Ticket Stubs, Old Documents, Heritage by KFD
Antique Mini Brads: by KFD

Anita cut the shutters to allow her ancestors to peek out the windows of the bedrooms where they lived as girls. The flap below opens to a life story.

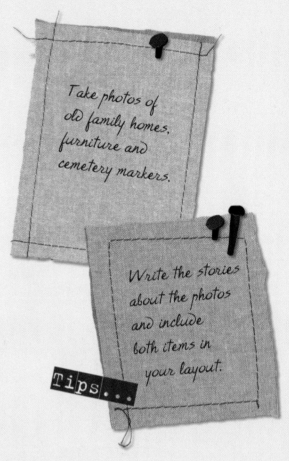

Take photos of old family homes, furniture and cemetery markers.

Write the stories about the photos and include both items in your layout.

Tips...

Old Churchyard
by Maureen Pinegar

Supplies
Papers: Days Gone By, by KFD
Stickers: Travel (sanded) by KFD
Embellishments:
by Making Memories
Rubber Stamps: unknown

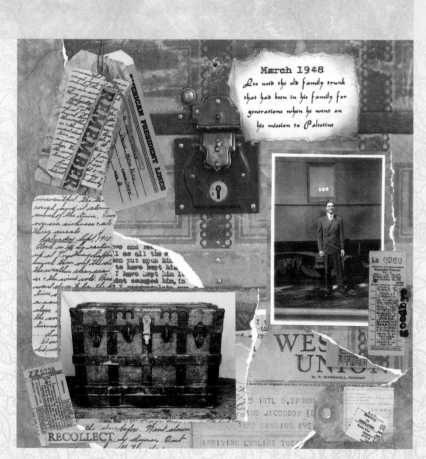

March 1948
Leo used the old family trunk that had been in his family for generations when he went on his mission to Palestine

Grandpa's Trunk
by Debra Wilcox

Supplies
Paper: Grandma's Trunk, Farewell Collage, Shabby Brown, Old Documents by KFD
Stickers: Remember, Old Ticket Stubs, Ancestry Definitions, Old Tags by KFD

heirlo

Carl August Hauser
by Joy Candrian

Supplies
Papers: Black Letter, Red Crackle, Shadow Box by KFD
Stickers: Alphabet Tags, Heritage by KFD
Cardstock: by Bazzill Basics
String

Joy made a small replica of Carl Hauser's passport including pages that turn. The writing on the layout describes her discovery of this ancestor while visiting Germany and contains information she learned about his life.

Joy's ancestor named his immigrant ship in his personal journal. A relative discovered a painting of the same ship at the National Maritime Museum in London. To research an immigrant ship from England, go online to www.nmm.ac.uk. Select "Collections & Research," then click on "Historic Photographs Catalogue." Other countries may have similar maritime information available on the Internet.

The Voyage
by Joy Candrian

Supplies

Paper: Grandfather's Journal, Shadow Box, Grandma's Trunk by KFD
Key Sticker: Heritage by KFD
Quotes: Journey Cut & Tear Quotes by KFD

Mesh: Making Memories
Photo Corners: Karen Foster Metals by KFD
Crystal Lacquer: by Sakura Hobby Craft

Tips...

Research area maps from an ancestor's time period. Scrapbook a comparison of then- and-now maps.

Research historical events that took place during the lives of your ancestors. This information may have influenced their life choices.

Never separate a series work like a multiple-page letter, journal, diary, pension, etc.

journals

Joy photocopied her ancestor's journal page to add a personal touch.

Journals of the Past
by Joy Candrian

Supplies

Papers: Antique Parchment, Parched Leather, Old Book Liner by KFD
Photo Corners and Key: Karen Foster Metals by KFD

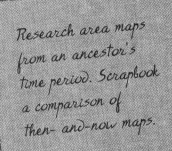

Tip...

The itinerary (opposite) describing the voyage was typed directly from journal pages such as the one on the right.

Journals of the past

George arrived in Utah in *1855* and settled in Farmington. In *1859*, he married *Emma Bond*. She bore him a son, George Bond Thatcher unfortunately she died less than a month later. In 1863, he married Emma's sister, Hannah Bond. She also had a son but both died during childbirth. On Nov. 9, *1864*, he married *Mary Rees* who immigrated from Wales and was 20 years younger than George. They had *14 children*. My grandfather, Wilford Earnest, was the youngest child of that family. George's journal documented all of the above information. The writing on the left is a page from his journal. This journal was given to my grandfather, then to my father, Wilford Everett Thatcher, and currently is in the possession of my oldest brother, Lester Don Thatcher of Oregon City, Oregon.

My Great-grandfather George Thatcher was born Nov. 6, 1824 in England. When...

Are **tre**asures of the future.

Marguerite's Shadow Box
by Jennifer Straus

Supplies
Paper: Shadow Box, Old Book Liner, Black Letter, Calligraphy Collage, Parish Records by KFD
Stickers: Old Documents, Old Alphabet, Ancestry Definitions, Old Ticket Stubs, Remember by KFD
Antique Bracelet: Jennifer's family heirloom

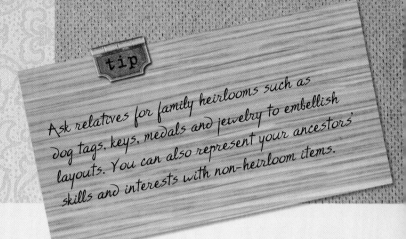

tip

Ask relatives for family heirlooms such as dog tags, keys, medals and jewelry to embellish layouts. You can also represent your ancestors' skills and interests with non-heirloom items.

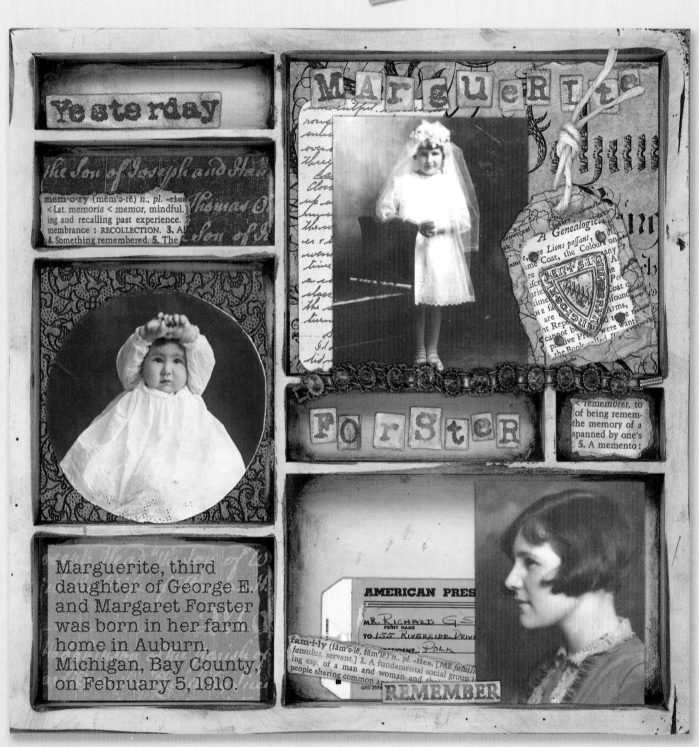

Grandmother's Treasures
by Karen Foster

Supplies
Papers: Grandma's Trunk by KFD
Quotes: Grandmothers
Cut & Tear Quotes by KFD
Embellishments: Jewelry
and sewing items

Grandmother's Treasures

*The old trunk
in the attic
Is ancient
and dusty,
And filled with
great treasures
Though yellowed
and musty.
There are lockets
and letters
And old dolls
with curls,
From days long ago
When Grandmas
were girls.*

tip

*To make the key
appear to hang from
the trunk latch, cut
the latch flap so it
lifts up. Glue cord
with key to the
chipboard underneath.*

research

Trip to England
by Jennifer Straus

Supplies
Paper: Old London, Shabby
Parchment by KFD
Stickers: Old Ticket Stubs,
Ancestry Definitions by KFD
Cardstock: by Bazzill Basics

Chapter 5

Ancestry Boxes

Some of your memorabilia may be too bulky for a scrapbook layout. Create ancestry boxes filled with these family treasures. You can also use the boxes as a place to showcase ancestry tribute books.

The farm journal inside this ancestry box shares space with heirlooms from the farm. Each piece is labeled with a tag to explain its importance. Stones in the bucket and box are a reminder of clearing the land by hand.

Instructions

1. To make farm journal (opposite), cut two pieces of cardstock 12" x 4" and 4" x 4". Tape together in a straight line. Fold into fourths lengthwise. Cover outside with Brown Leather paper. Cover inside with School Stripe paper (left) and Brown Leather paper (right). Decorate with Saddle Up stickers.

2. On left flap, attach vellum pocket with stickers and antique brads. Cut cardstock tag and cover with Brown Leather paper. Add journaling and fibers.

3. Cut one piece of cardstock 6" x 3½". Fold in half (3" x 3½"). Cover outside with Brown Leather paper and inside with Dusty Rose Crackle paper. Cut window in bottom half. Sketch window and wood grain. Attach with antique brads to one of the center squares of the 16" x 4" piece. Adhere photo under window flap.

4. At bottom of center square, attach 12" x 3½" piece of Shadow Box paper. Line the back side with another paper if desired. Write a story here. Accordion-fold paper to fit center square. Chalk edges if desired. Add photos and/or journaling to other flaps.

5. Decorate farm box with paper, stickers and garden tools, etc. Line inside with Old Script paper.

Stories from the farm about Grandpa's buckets of rocks

Chalk background papers on each flap before attaching photographs. When folded closed, the journal can be tied with old cotton cord or frayed fibers.

Tip...

Farm Journal and Box
by Caroll Shreeve

Supplies
Cardstock: by Bazzill Basics
Vellum: Visions
Paper: Shadow Box, Brown Leather, School Stripe, Dusty Rose Crackle, Old Script, Shabby Parchment by KFD
Stickers: Saddle Up, Heritage by KFD
Pencils: by Prismacolor
Rusty Box, Bucket, Garden Tools: by Darice
Eyelet Frame: by Woo Hoo Wowies
Black Mini Brads: by KFD

When the inside flap is lifted, it reveals the vignette of iron skillets and the explanation of their importance on the farm. Below the skillets, a window cut out of another flap reveals Caroll's father and uncle on horseback. Vellum pockets hold tags with photo captions.

Supplies
Box with Hinges and Latch
(3 ¹/₄" high x 8 ¹/₄" wide x 5 ³/₄" deep)
Paper: Dark Green Crackle, Antique Lace, Antique Leather by KFD
Stickers: Remember by KFD

Ancestry
Boxes

Caroll painted all the edges of the box inside and out with stripes of metallic gold and copper paint. She then glued scrapbook papers and stickers onto the rest of the box.

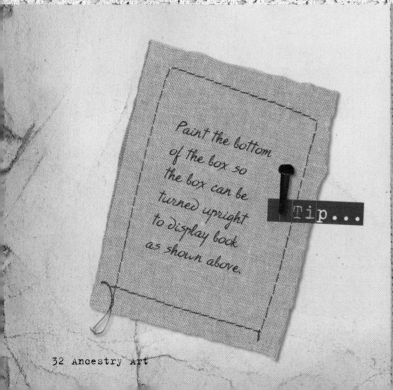

Paint the bottom of the box so the box can be turned upright to display book as shown above.

Tip...

Instructions
Chest

1. Enlarge trunk pattern to 12" x 12". Enlarge flap proportionately. Make extra copy of pattern. Cut trunk from chipboard, then cut pattern into sections (side, front and back) along inner dashed lines. Cut trunk lid and front from from one sheet of Grandma's Trunk paper, centering printed images in correct positions. Cut out back, sides and bottom from another sheet of Grandma's Trunk paper. Allow ½" around these pieces for overlap.

2. Score chipboard on dashed lines and fold. Glue trunk paper to chipboard overlapping edges. Attach lid with hinges. Add mini brads. Line trunk with additional paper cut from pattern if desired.

Treasure Booklet

1. Fold cover and inside pages in half. Stitch pages together at center-fold line. Glue stitched pages into fold of book cover.

2. Decorate cover with Heritage stickers and Cut & Tear Quotes. Fill pages with photos, documents, ephemera and life stories. Keep booklet inside treasure box.

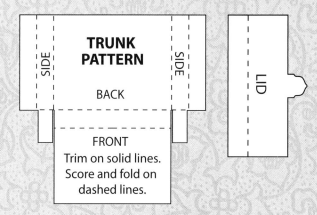

TRUNK PATTERN

SIDE

SIDE

LID

BACK

FRONT
Trim on solid lines.
Score and fold on dashed lines.

Treasure Chest and Booklet
by Judy Koreck

Supplies
Paper: Grandma's Trunk by KFD
Gold Mini Brads: by KFD
Hinges and Embellishments: Karen Foster Metals by KFD
Stickers: Heritage by KFD
Quote: Heritage Cut & Tear Quotes by KFD
Mesh: Magic Mesh

Heirloom Boxes
by Wayne Dieleman

Supplies
Boxes: Wayne hand made two fabric-covered boxes and covered them with paper: (2½" high x 9¼" wide x 5" deep)
Papers: Old Documents, Genealogy Collage, Grandma's Trunk, Shabby Parchment by KFD
Embellishments: Karen Foster Metals by KFD

Wayne's small ancestry books are kept inside these boxes.

Wedding Heirloom Box

by Caroll Shreeve

Supplies

Box with Hinged Lid and Clasp
Paper and Vellum: Wedding Collage, Parish Records, Red Crackle, Old Script by KFD
Stickers: Old Tags, Old Ticket Stubs, Remember, Travel, Wedding by KFD
Embellishments: Karen Foster Metals by KFD and Caroll's personal heirlooms

Fill box with an ancestor's wedding heirlooms and wedding certificate.

Instructions:

1. Glue four round wooden balls to bottom of box for feet.

2. Paint edges of box and feet with metallic gold paint.

3. Remove latch and affix scrapbook papers to inside and outside box surfaces.

4. Replace latch.

5. Layer tags with paper, stickers and gold paint.

6. Curve tags by rolling around a pencil and attach to lid with ribbons and gold cord.

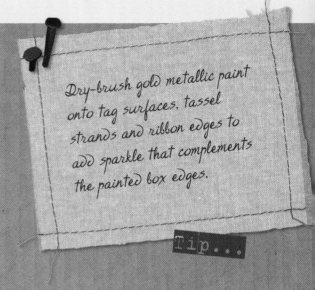

Dry-brush gold metallic paint onto tag surfaces, tassel strands and ribbon edges to add sparkle that complements the painted box edges.

Tip...

Create a box to hold a set of small ancestry books. Each book contains a life story and special memories.

(See instructions on page 37.)

Ancestry Boxes

Tips...

To fit a wedding certificate in the box, reduce it on a copier and decorate.

Make a gate-folded cover for a miniature certificate. The piece below is shown open on the opposite page.

Wedding Certificate
by Joy Candrian

Supplies
Paper: Parish Records by KFD
Stickers: Heritage by KFD
Antique Mini Brad: by KFD
Eyelets: by Making Memories
Rubber Stamps: by Hero Arts, Raindrops and Roses
Real Postmarks and Stamps

Chapter 6

Ancestry Books

Handmade or altered books containing life stories of your ancestors will become keepsakes for generations. They can be made to read like storybooks or be filled with interactive pockets, tags and memorabilia.

Judy's handmade life story books about her maternal grandparents and great-grandparents, have become a treasure for her family.

Treasure Book Series
by Judy Ezola

Handmade Books

Supplies

Paper: Shabby Dark, Old Book Liner, Red Crackle, Antique Lace, Old Book Cover, Shabby Map, Immigrant Collage, Wedding Collage, Soft Green Crackle, Dusty Rose Crackle, Grandma's Trunk, Life Story Continued by KFD

Stickers: Old Tags by KFD
Quotes: Journey Cut & Tear Quotes by KFD
Embellishments: Karen Foster Metals by KFD

Instructions for One Book

1. Cut one piece of chipboard to 9 1/2" x 6".

2. Score two vertical fold marks to create 3/8" - wide spine.

3. Cover with scrapbook papers and fold chipboard into book shape.

4. Cut six pieces of Life Story Continued paper to 9" x 5 7/8".

5. Cut two pieces of Old Book Liner paper to 9" x 5 7/8" (these will become the two end-sheets for each book).

6. Fold sheets in half to 4 1/2" x 5 7/8" with printed side in. Stack folded sheets so the folds are lined up on one side. Place folded Old Book Liner sheets on the top and bottom of stack. Glue wrong sides of the folded half-pages together. Each two halves glued together becomes a page of the book.

7. Center the folds of prepared book pages into the spine.

8. Glue outer front and back pages of Old Book Liner to inside front covers as end sheets. Glue ribbon ties inside end-sheets.

9. Journal a life story within and decorate.

To Make Box

1. To hold this book series, make a box out of chipboard 6 1/4" high x 2 3/4" wide x 4 5/8" deep.

2. Cover with scrapbook papers, wrapping as you would a gift.

3. Glue paper in place.

4. Allow 1" of extra scrapbook paper to fold and glue inside the open area of the box for sturdiness and a finished appearance.

5. Decorate with ribbon, a tag and metal embellishments.

Read your life story books to children as bedtime stories.

To create a set of coordinating books, design similar covers and choose matching papers to decorate the insides.

Tips...

remembrance

Joy's Tribute to Her Mother

Accordion Booklet
by Joy Candrian

Supplies

Papers: Life Story, School Stripe, Shabby Dark, Red Stitched by KFD
Quotes: Mothers Cut & Tear Quotes by KFD
Stickers: Remember by KFD
Cut & Tear Bingo Cards: by KFD
Netting: by The Robin's Nest
Beads and Copper Wire: by Westrim Crafts
Copper Trim: by Venture Tape
Antique Mini Brads: by KFD
Pastel Mini Buttons (White): by KFD
Terrifically Tacky Tape: by Art Accents for Provo Craft
Fiber: unknown
Tags

Instructions

This accordion booklet is pictured in the window box on p. 32.

1. Cut one sheet of Shabby Dark paper to 10" x 12". Fold in half to 5" x 12". Fold in half again to 5" x 6" and then again to 5" x 3". Spread sheet out then fold accordion-style. Open again and lay flat. This sheet makes eight panels (see Section B, opposite).

2. Cut another sheet to 10" x 6" and fold in half to 5" x 6". Fold in half again to 5" x 3". Spread sheet out then fold accordion-style. Open again and lay flat. This sheet makes four panels (see Section A, opposite).

3. Prepare pockets to fit the 3" panels (see opposite). Stitch into place with sewing machine or by hand.

4. Join the two sections of accordion paper with strong tape on reverse side (see opposite).

5. Finish edges of netting with copper tape.

6. Fold entire piece in half lengthwise with reverse sides together, then fold into accordion shape.

7. Cover some tags with Red Stitched or School Stripe paper and re-cut tag holes.

8. Age tags and Cut & Tear Quotes by crumpling and chalking. Decorate tags and book with photos, journaling, reduced-size documents, buttons, lace, brads, etc.

9. Finish all outer edges with copper foil tape. Smooth copper edges with bone folder.

Double-sided paper is ideal for pockets that fold over at the top.

Assembly Directions

1. On the reverse side, align the panel sections so the edges, fold and corners meet exactly. Do not overlap.

2. Attach sections A and B with Terrifically Tacky Tape running the length of the seam.

3. Press firmly to secure in place.

4. Fold piece in half horizontally with reverse sides together.

5. Fold accordion-style.

6. Tuck tags into pockets.

Accordion books can be viewed from either side with all stitching hidden on the inside.

Section A

Section B

Section A

Section B

When pockets have been stitched and sections are taped together, fold reverse-sides together on this line.

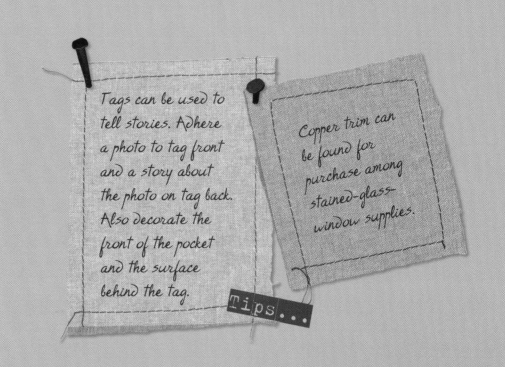

Tags can be used to tell stories. Adhere a photo to tag front and a story about the photo on tag back. Also decorate the front of the pocket and the surface behind the tag.

Copper trim can be found for purchase among stained-glass-window supplies.

Tips...

Pay tribute to an ancestor by creating an altered book displayed in a decorative box. This small altered book makes an intriguing conversation piece or gift.

Grandma Mary Rose

by Joy Candrian

Instructions

1. Use craft knife to remove shiny commercial surface of diary. Sand lightly to allow it to accept glue and scrapbook paper.

2. Remove pages from book and create new pages by a hand-sewing a running stitch to attach pages together from behind.

3. Glue folded edge of pages into the inside back of the hardbound diary cover.

4. Decorate the book with journaling, photos and copies of documents that have been reduced in size.

5. Create pockets to hold tags decorated with the above-mentioned items.

6. Decorate cover with ribbon and metal frame.

7. Create tag bookmark using locket or bezel. Fold ribbon in half. Tuck through hole in tag. Pull loose ends of ribbon through hole in bezel and tie knot.

Supplies

Locking Diary: Thrift store
Paper: Old Book Liner, Parched Leather, Shadow Box, Shabby Map, Map Collage, Shabby Dark, Grandfather's Journal, Parish Records, Burgundy Crackle, Black Letter by KFD
Stickers: Remember by KFD
Embellishments: Karen Foster Metals by KFD

heirloom books

Tear pockets at various angles before adhering to the pages of your book. This creates interest and variety in the design.

Postage stamps need not be old to use them as ephemera. Choose stamps that are postmarked if possible. Sand slightly and add chalk to age.

To create a bezel for your bookmark, remove stone from an old piece of cheap jewelry. Replace it with a photo of an ancestor. Apply water-based clear lacquer over the top of the photo. Allow to dry.

My Father, My Friend

Richard G. Sharp

Front cover

Dad was born April 29, 1920 in Salt Lake City, Utah. He was the oldest of five children born to my grandparents, June B. and Ida Giles Sharp. He grew up and lived on Windsor Street near 13th South where he remembers going to Liberty Park to play in the summer and to ice skate in the winter. His family didn't have much money, and when he was about six years old and starting school, Grandma made him wear girl boots with fur on top to school. Those were the only boots they had for him. He was so embarrassed, but he pretended he was Santa Claus with fur on his boots so he wouldn't feel silly. As a young man, when World War II started, he enlisted in the Army, but fortunately never had to leave the U.S. He became a pilot and then an airplane mechanic.

Inside front cover

true love joy
forever
faithful friends
heart prayers
family sweet
home people

Page 4

My Father,
My Friend
by Judy Ezola

Supplies
Paper: Old Book Liner, Shadow Box, Parish Records, Grandma's Trunk, Shabby Map by KFD
Stickers: Remember, Old Documents, Old Ticket Stubs by KFD
Antique Mini Brads: by KFD
Metal Clip: by Making Memories

A cut-down portion of the Shadow Box paper makes an easy-to-design book cover.

A tribute book should portray the personality and character of your loved one.

Tips...

When my father was a little boy...

The most important thing a father can do for his children is to love their mother.

REMEMBER

Photos arranged chronologically from childhood to retirement-age make this book a photo story.

Dear Old Dad

After the war Dad went to school at U.S.C. studying architecture on the G.I. bill. Before he left for California and during his student years, he courted my mother. She wasn't interested at first, but absence must truly make the heart grow fonder because she finally said "yes" to him in a telegram she sent to him while he was away at college. He immediately dropped out of school and came home to marry her. In spite of not graduating, he became a draftsman and then started his own successful architecture business. My brothers and sisters and I came along and he became the proud father of seven children. He says that marrying Mom was the best thing that ever happened to him. Dad has always been a man of integrity and honor, a legacy which he leaves to his children and grandchildren.

tribute books

Mini Book
(above and below)

by Wayne Dieleman

Supplies

Paper: Grandma's Trunk, Deep Green Crackle, Grandfather's Journal, Shabby Map Shabby Parchment by KFD
Cream Cardstock: by Club Scrap
Stickers: Remember, Old Alphabet, Travel by KFD
Quotes: Mothers and Fathers Cut & Tear Quotes by KFD

tips

To give the look of nailheads on the book, Wayne tore a strip from Grandma's Trunk paper which features a piece of wood containing rivets.

Dry-brush metallic colors onto black wire bindings to make them less industrial-looking.

Wayne's pages are filled with mini documents, tags, pockets, journaling and photos of both parents in their teenage years, and when they met and married.

Instructions for White Booklet: (opposite page)

1. Cut cardstock to 9 ¾" x 3 ½".

2. Score and fold at the 3 ½", 4", 7 ¾" and 8 ¼" marks. The area between the 3 ½" and 4" dimensions is the spine.

3. To create inside pages, cut double-sided sheets of paper to 6 ¾" x 3 ¾". Fold each sheet in half. Stack folded sheets with folds facing one side. Glue folds into the spine of the book or stitch folds to book-binder's tape and adhere to spine.

4. Create flap by the fold at the 8 ¼" mark.

5. To close, fold short flap over the body of the booklet.

6. Wrap with a cord.

Pieter Jan Dieleman Book (above and opposite)
by Wayne Dieleman

Supplies
Double Wire-Bound Book (5 ¾" x 8", folding in from both sides): Handmade by Wayne
Paper: Parched Leather, Deep Green Crackle, Grandfather's Journal, Shabby Map, Shabby Brown, Shabby Parchment by KFD
Stickers: Old Alphabet, Remember by KFD

fold-out books

My Family Legacy Trunk Book

The trunk book cover opens at the latch. The top layer of this trunk book folds up while the bottom layer folds down. The bottom flap is attached to the background with a hinge of tape. Pages inside are attached with brads under the top flap.

The double pocket on the inside was created by folding a tuck into a 12" x 12" sheet of Old Scroll paper. Brads were used to secure the pocket tuck and to attach the pocket to the page.

While Grandma's Trunk paper makes a beautiful interactive scrapbook layout, it can also be used to cover the sides of a 12" x 12" x 12" box in which to store family history documents for safekeeping.

My Family Legacy
by Caroll Shreeve

Supplies

Paper: Grandma's Trunk, Old Scroll, Military Collage, Parched Leather, Gold Crackle by KFD
Stickers: Heritage, Old Documents by KFD
Antique Mini Brads: by KFD
Latch: by KFD

Instructions

1. For a sturdy background, cover 12" x 12" chipboard with paper.

2. Tape top and bottom chipboard-backed flaps in place with bookbinder's tape.

3. Cover tape with Gold Crackle paper.

4. Attach pages under lid with mini brads.

5. Create and attach pockets and decorate.

6. Attach metal latch to upper and lower flaps.

with pockets

Little Memory Books

Little memory books can be filled with the mementos and memories of one special event such as a vacation, a high school reunion, or a wedding. It can also commemorate a series of events that relate to each other such as several childhood memories.

Fresh Fish Notebook
by Caroll Shreeve

Supplies
Paper: Light Blue Weathered Wood, Teal Weathered Wood, Light Green Weathered Wood by KFD
Stickers: Home Sweet Home, Old Rooster Café by KFD
Fibers: by Darice
Ribbon and Chopsticks: unknown
Light Blue Mini Brads: by KFD
Metallic Rub Ons: by Craf-T Products

Instructions
1. Cut chipboard to 9 ½" x 5".

2. Fold 4½" for front and back and ½" for spine.

3. Cut a notch 2" high x 1½" wide in the right front corner.

4. Cover all surfaces with scrapbook paper.

5. Rub metallic cream on decorative elements on front cover and inside back cover.

6. Cut desired number of inside pages 8 ½" x 3".

7. Fold pages in half, stitch, glue to inside spine.

This chopstick holder can be adjusted to hold heirloom items such as a spoon, glasses or pocket knife.

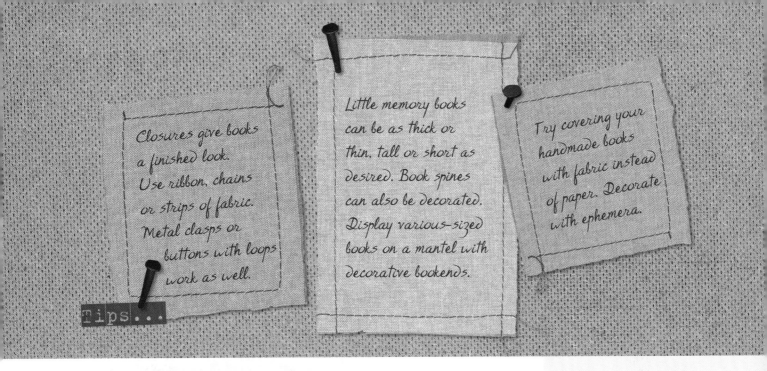

Closures give books a finished look. Use ribbon, chains or strips of fabric. Metal clasps or buttons with loops work as well.

Little memory books can be as thick or thin, tall or short as desired. Book spines can also be decorated. Display various-sized books on a mantel with decorative bookends.

Try covering your handmade books with fabric instead of paper. Decorate with ephemera.

Home Sweet Home
by Caroll Shreeve

Supplies
Paper: Gold Weathered Wood, Checkered Weathered Wood by KFD
Stickers: Old Rooster Café, Home Sweet Home, Childhood Clear Quotes by KFD
Black Mini Brads: by KFD
Chain and Button: Karen Foster Metals by KFD

Instructions
1. Follow directions on opposite page, but do not notch front cover.

2. Make the inside pages 8 ¼" x 5 ¼" before folding them in half.

3. Continue with directions on opposite page.

This book contains Caroll's memory of a special summer spent with her grandmother on the farm.

book of memories

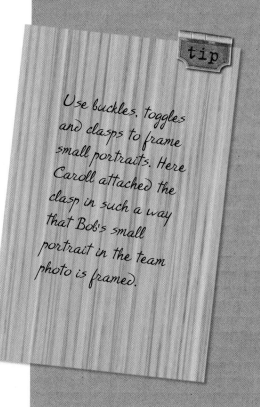

tip

Use buckles, toggles and clasps to frame small portraits. Here Caroll attached the clasp in such a way that Bob's small portrait in the team photo is framed.

Bob's Batting Record
by Caroll Shreeve

Supplies
Papers: Baseball Periodical, Maroon Jersey by KFD
Cardstock: by Bazzill Basics
Stickers: Baseball Definitions, Varsity Alphabet by KFD
Embellishments: Karen Foster Metals by KFD
Fibers: by Darice; Making Memories
Antique and Black Mini Brads: by KFD

Books can be saddle-stitched (tied at the spine, as above) or perfect-bound (see Wayne's mini book on p. 44). Saddle-stitched books work well as thin books and perfect-bound books work well as thicker books.

Theme Books

Little memory books are easy to create and are ideal to give as gifts commemorating special occasions. In this format, small pages can be designed quickly using photographs, journaling and memorabilia. Word stickers can be used as headers or page titles.

tips

The subject in your photo can appear to be positioned behind a window. To create this effect, slice a copy of your photo vertically or both vertically and horizontally. Slide the pieces slightly apart.

Adhere foam dots behind the basketball sticker to give it a three-dimensional look.

theme books

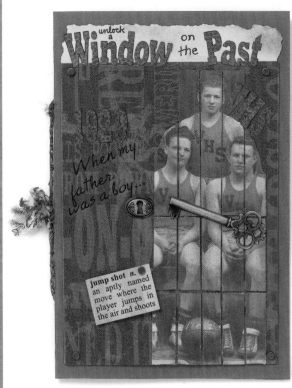

unlock a **Window** *on the* **Past**

When my father was a boy...

jump shot *n.* an aptly named move where the player jumps in the air and shoots

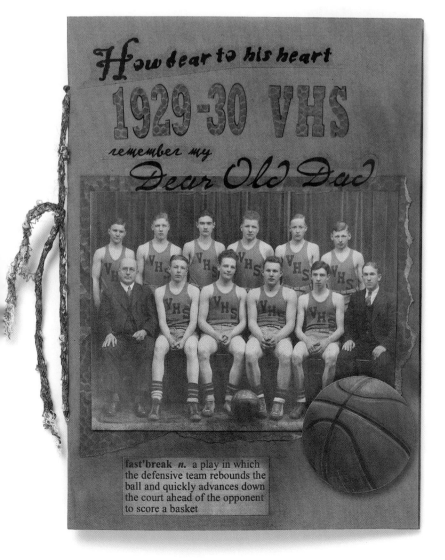

How dear to his heart

1929-30 VHS

remember my

Dear Old Dad

fast'break *n.* a play in which the defensive team rebounds the ball and quickly advances down the court ahead of the opponent to score a basket

Vaughnsville Champs
by Caroll Shreeve

Supplies
Paper: Free Throw by KFD
Cardstock: by Bazzill Basics
Stickers: Basketball Alphabet, Fathers Clear Quotes, Basketball Definitions by KFD

Dad's 1929 Basketball Team
by Caroll Shreeve

Supplies
Paper: Slam Dunk by KFD
Cardstock: by Bazzill Basics
Stickers: Basketball Alphabet, Fathers Clear Quotes, Basketball Definitions by KFD

More Ancestry *Art*

Creating ancestry scrapbooks and theme books will inspire the desire to continue using old photos and documents in artistic ways. These creations are illustrations for your ancestry life stories.

3D Shadow Boxes

by Caroll Shreeve and Karen Foster

For instructions to make your own 3D shadow box, see p. 67

Supplies (large box)

Paper: Old Script, Purple Crackle, Parched Leather by KFD

Quotes: Mothers and Grandfathers Cut & Tear Quotes by KFD

Embellishments: Karen Foster Metals by KFD

Supplies (small box)

Paper: Mustard Weathered Wood, Checked Weathered Wood, Light Blue Weathered Wood, Cream Weathered Wood by KFD

Embellishments: Karen Foster Metals by KFD

Recollect Card
by Bonnette Aalders

Supplies
Paper: Old Book Liner, Grandfather's Journal by KFD
Dark Brown and Pale Yellow Cardstock: by Bazzill Basics
Stickers: Remember by KFD

Create beautiful tribute books by filling 6" x 6" scrapbook binders with small ancestry layouts. The small envelope on this layout holds a reduced copy of a keepsake letter.

Antique cards add a homespun warmth. The message inside reads: "Thank you, Grandma, for starting me out right."

Life Is Good Card & Envelope
by Karen Foster

Supplies
Paper: Old Script, Parish Records, Shabby Brown by KFD
Quotes: Life Cut & Tear Quotes by KFD
Antique Mini Brads: by KFD
Chalk

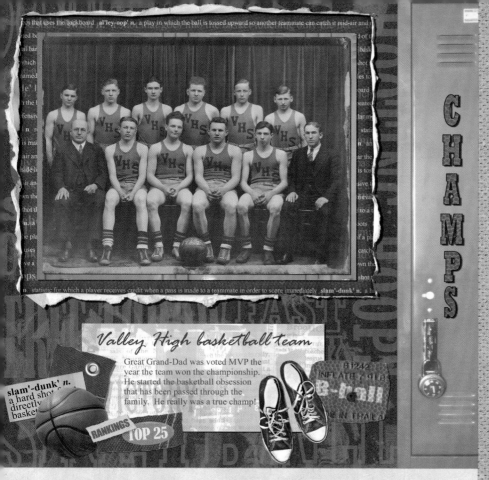

C H A M P S

tips

To create rolled window, follow directions on p. 76. However, allow room around photo in this layout for two inner mats of contrasting color.

Valley High basketball team

Great Grand-Dad was voted MVP the year the team won the championship. He started the basketball obsession that has been passed through the family. He really was a true champ!

slam'-dunk' n. a hard shot directly basket

RANKINGS TOP 25

Valley High Basketball Team

by Sarah Treu

Supplies

Paper: Lockers, Free Throw, Basketball Talk, Basketball Collage by KFD
Stickers: Basketball, Basketball Alphabet, Basketball Definitions by KFD

Attach locker to layout on the right side, allowing left side to lift open. Write additional journaling inside.

ACTIVE DUTY

Harvey L. Ludlow
Served in Pacific Theater,
World War II
1942-1945

Active Duty

by Sarah Treu

Supplies

Paper: Khaki Brown Stitched, Army Green Stitched, Military Collage by KFD
Stickers: Military by KFD

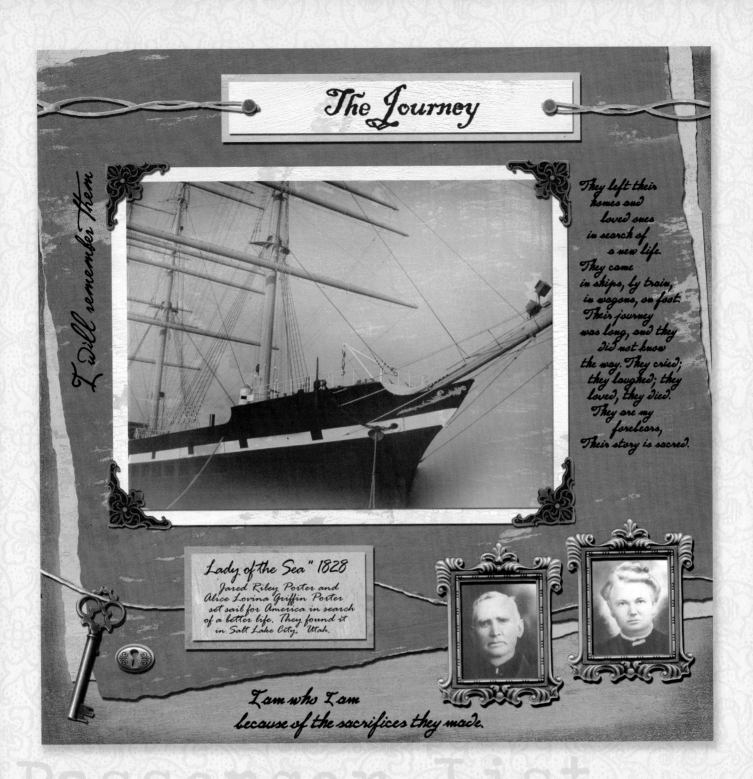

The Journey

I will remember them

They left their homes and loved ones in search of a new life. They came in ships, by train, in wagons, on foot. Their journey was long, and they did not know the way. They cried; they laughed; they loved, they died. They are my forebears. Their story is sacred.

"Lady of the Sea" 1828
Jared Riley Porter and Alice Lovina Griffin Porter set sail for America in search of a better life. They found it in Salt Lake City, Utah.

I am who I am because of the sacrifices they made.

Passenger List

The Journey
by Sarah Treu

Supplies
Paper: Teal Weathered Wood, Cream Weathered Wood, Mustard Weathered Wood, Light Green Weathered Wood by KFD
Stickers: Journey Clear Quotes by KFD
Embellishments: Karen Foster Metals by KFD

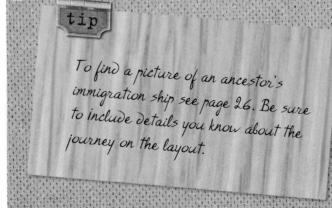

tip

To find a picture of an ancestor's immigration ship see page 26. Be sure to include details you know about the journey on the layout.

Dear Old Dad

Dear Old Dad Card
by Trisha Riches

Supplies
Paper: Cinnamon Stick,
Shabby Parchment by KFD
Stickers: Old Tags, Remember by KFD
Quotes: Fathers Cut & Tear Quotes by KFD

Bonnette accented the beautiful calligraphy in this layout by cutting out portions of Calligraphy Collage Paper, matting it in dark brown cardstock and adhering it with double-stick foam tape.

Christmas Morning
by Bonnette Aalders

Supplies
Paper:
Calligraphy Collage, Old
Documents, Shabby
Parchment by KFD
White Vellum:
unknown
Stickers:
Old Documents by KFD
Dark Brown Cardstock:
by Bazzill Basics
Photo Mat:
Part of original photo

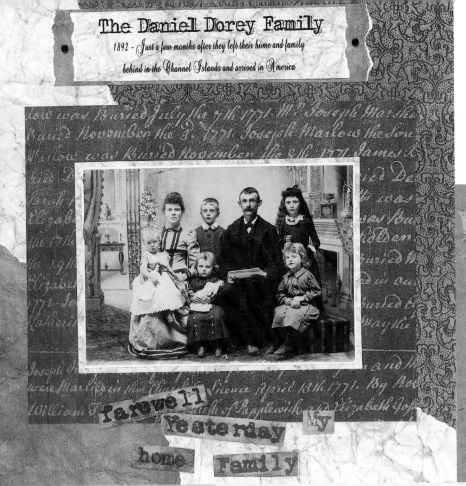

The Daniel Dorey Family

1892 - Just a few months after they left their home and family behind in the Channel Islands and arrived in America

Farewell Yesterday my home Family

The Daniel Dorey Family

by Debra Wilcox

Supplies

Paper: Old Book Liner, Parish Records, Shabby Parchment, Shabby Brown by KFD
Stickers: Remember by KFD
Black Mini Brads: by KFD

Tip...

Place a photo of yourself or your children on the trunk of the family tree with parents directly above. Place the photos of paternal grandparents and great-grandparents on one side and maternal on the other. Write the names under each photo.

Don't discard unidentifiable photos. Arrange them just for fun anywhere on Family Tree paper to create a beautiful work of art.

Family Tree

by Karen Foster

Supplies

Paper:
Parish Records,
Family Tree by KFD
Quotes:
Heritage Cut &
Tear Quotes by KFD

...And I will turn the hearts of the fathers to their children and the hearts of the children to their fathers... Malachi 4:6

family tree

Debra created symmetrical pillars of torn paper holding up the arch across the top. This formal design is reminiscent of the serious expressions on the faces in the photo.

Clyde Harley Wilcox
by Debra Wilcox

Supplies
Paper: Black Letter, Shabby Brown by KFD
Stickers: Old Documents by KFD
Cardstock: by Bazzill Basics
Photo Corners: unknown

vital records

Clyde Harley Wilcox
3 year Swiss/German
Mission
1922 ✦ 1924

13. Sept. 1752. Sammonn

The wedding of Pieter Jan Dieleman and Chatharina Suzanna Dronkers...

Easter 1947 my Father met my Mother in Amsterdam during a day of the Young Church. They fell in Love that summer and on May 13 1948 the married in the Church of Nisse.

My Parents' Wedding
by Wayne Dieleman

Supplies
Paper: Immigrant Collage, Shabby Parchment by KFD
Textured Olive Paper: by Club Scrap
Heart Stickers: by Magenta
Rubber Stamp Clock: by Magenta
Heart Brads: by Making Memories
Chalk Ink: Olive Pastel by ColorBox
Font: FanciHand
Cardstock: by Bazzill Basics

Baby Jack 1902
by Judy Koreck

Supplies
Paper: Shadow Box, Old Book Liner, Shabby Brown by KFD
Brown Cardstock: by Bazzill Basics
Stickers: Old Alphabet, Old Tags, Old Ticket Stubs by KFD
Quotes: Life and Heritage Cut & Tear Quotes by KFD

Matting design elements in a thin edge of ebony cardstock (above) adds class to layouts that need to be dressed up.

Tip...

Line some of the shadow box sections with various aged-toned papers allowing corner shadows to remain visible. This technique adds depth to your layout.

Where there is love there is life. Gandhi

Days gone by

JACK

1902

When my father
was a little boy...

tip

To create the rectangular design on the left, mat progressively smaller rectangles with narrow cardstock mat. Add row of brads and envelope.

When My Father
Was a Little Boy

by Judy Koreck

Supplies

Paper: Calligraphy Collage, Old Book Liner, Shabby Dark, Shabby Brown by KFD
Stickers: Old Ticket Stubs by KFD
Quotes: Fathers Cut & Tear Quotes by KFD
Antique Mini Brads: by KFD

Growing Up

by Jennifer Straus

Supplies

Paper: Old Book Cover, Shabby Parchment, Shabby Brown by KFD
White Vellum: unknown
Stickers: Remember, Alphabet Tags, Ancestry Definitions by KFD

Include favorite pets, old furniture and well-loved playing spots to evoke memories beyond words.

Just a normal mid-western kid, Jim spe his days enjoying li He is seated here wi his trusty companion Petey, standing on a rock at Island Lake the Upper Penninsula and riding his bike, delivering the morning papers.

best friend imagine remember forever

his·to·ry (hĭs'tə-rē) n., pl. -ries. [Lat. learned man.] 1. A narrative of past even

G r o w i n g U p

Little Girl Reading

by Debra Wilcox

Supplies

Paper: Old Book Cover, Grandfather's Journal, Shadow Box, Old Script by KFD
Ribbon and Buttons: unknown

old book cover idea

The Good Old Days
by Jennifer Straus

Supplies

Paper: Shadow Box, Old Script, Genealogy Collage, Old Book Liner, Shabby Brown by KFD
Stickers: Old Tags by KFD
Quotes: Grandfathers Cut & Tear Quotes by KFD
Cut Outs: Bingo Cards and Domino by KFD

In the good old Days when grandpa's were boys they didn't own a lot of toys. But they always had their fun playing Games like Run Sheep Run, pitching pennies, playing jacks, collecting cards by the stacks, marbles, Bingo, dominoes too, Grandpa's had fun just like you.

The Good Old Days

Lee and Mary often enjoyed game playing. Both had a competitive spirit, and passed it on to me. I especially remember Friday nights. That was pot-luck Bingo night at the county hall. Even though I was too young to play Bingo, they took me along to play with the other kids. Those evenings were full of laughter, good friends and good food.

Remember
by Jennifer Straus

Supplies

Paper: Grandfather's Journal, Black Letter by KFD
White Vellum: unknown
Stickers: Old Alphabet, Remember, Old Tags by KFD

REMEMBER

father

He grew up in central Michigan with three sisters and a little brother who was 15 years younger. He was the oldest child in the family. They lived in a white two-story house with plenty of trees in the yard. His father, an attorney, enjoyed hunting and spending time outside in the woods. He took after his father. In school, he did about average, and went on to follow his father as an attorney. His family was always in church on Sunday and they had lots of close neighbors whom they spent hours playing cards, checkers and cribbage with. It was a good time to grow up. And now we enjoy looking at these photos his mom took with her old black and white 35mm camera. She even developed the images herself.

Dad

CHILDHOOD

Yesterday family

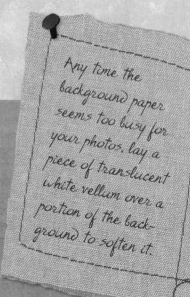

My Dad
6"x6" Layout Series
by Judy Koreck

Supplies
Paper: Shabby Brown, Immigrant Collage by KFD
Cardstock: by Bazzill Basics
Stickers: Old Alphabet by KFD
Antique Mini Brads: by KFD
Metal Star: by Making Memories

Evie
DuFour
Dorey
1906

To create a dimensional background, combine two coordinating papers to make one 11" x 11" square. Mat with a thin contrasting edge and place on a 12" x 12" coordinating background.

Tip...

Grace Dorey
by Debra Wilcox

Supplies
Paper: Winter Tapestry Brown, Shabby Dark, Snowflake Tapestry Brown, Snow Scene Tapestry by KFD
Stickers: Alphabet Tags by KFD
Antique Mini Brads: by KFD

He cheers me up
when things
are hard
and makes me
work **out** in
the yard.
He likes to
give too much
advice;
but even so
he's pretty nice.
He plays with
me and acts
so funny,
and sometimes
even gives
me money.
He's the BEST—
and I'm so glad
I have a
super kind
of **grandpa**

Grandpa
by Judy Koreck

Supplies

Paper: Parish Records,
Shabby Brown by KFD
Stickers: Old Documents by KFD
Quotes: Fathers and Grandfathers
Cut & Tear Quotes by KFD
Antique Mini Brads: by KFD

tips

A row of mini brads
in a narrow column
adds a touch of
class to your layout.

Tear and burn the edges
of the background paper to
create an aged look. Add
chalk if desired.

Father Frame
by Wayne Dieleman

Supplies
Paper: Grandma's Trunk by KFD
Walnut Ink: by Seven Gypsies
Writing Stamp: by Hero Arts
Key Stamp: by Magenta
Chalk Ink: Creamy Brown, Dark
Brown by ColorBox

frames

tip

To create an antique frame, sponge walnut ink onto unfinished wood. When dry, add rubber-stamped images. Decorate with cut paper elements.

Home Sweet Home
by Karen Foster

Supplies
Paper: Light Blue Weathered Wood, Gold Weathered Wood, Red Weathered Wood by KFD
Stickers: Childhood Clear Quotes, Home Sweet Home by KFD
Metal Corners: Karen Foster Metals by KFD

Karen Foster with her siblings. Karen is the baby on the left.

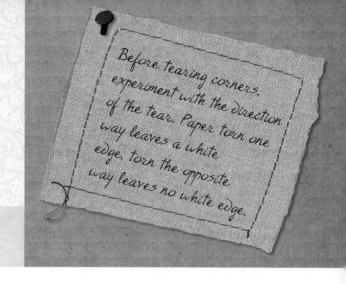

Before tearing corners, experiment with the direction of the tear. Paper torn one way leaves a white edge, torn the opposite way leaves no white edge.

family search

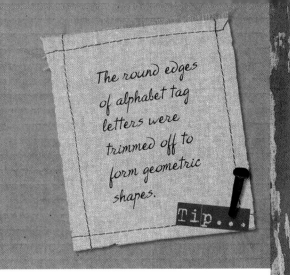

The round edges of alphabet tag letters were trimmed off to form geometric shapes.

Tip...

Mother
by Karen Foster

Supplies
Paper: Teal Weathered Wood, Light Blue Weathered Wood, Mustard Weathered Wood, Red Weathered Wood, Cream Weathered Wood by KFD
Stickers: Mother Clear Quotes, Alphabet Tags by KFD
Embellishments: Karen Foster Metals by KFD
Antique Mini Brads: by KFD

Handmade
Shadow Box
by Andrea Burgon

Supplies
3D Shadow Box: Handmade
Paper: Light Blue Weathered Wood, Gold Weathered Wood, Mustard Weathered Wood by KFD
Stickers: Childhood Clear Quotes by KFD
Embellishments: Karen Foster Metals by KFD

This 3D shadow box can be built by gluing easy-to-cut balsa wood pieces together. Build box sections as desired. Paint with tan tole paint. Sponge diluted dark brown tole paint into corners and along edges.

Homecoming '57

 Bebop

SODA SPRINGS HIGH

THE FIFTIES

Rock-N-Roll

ROCK-N-ROLL

The Swing

Homecoming '57
by Judy Ezola

Supplies
Paper: Nifty Fifties, Fifties Collage, Sock Hop, Records by KFD
Stickers: Fifties Phrases, The Fifties, Fifties Font by KFD

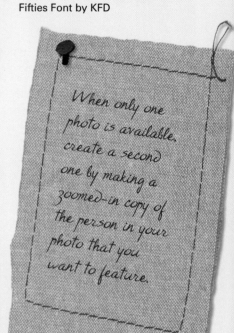

When only one photo is available, create a second one by making a zoomed-in copy of the person in your photo that you want to feature.

The Cool '50s
by Caroll Shreeve

Supplies
Paper: Nifty Fifties, Records, Sock Hop by KFD
Cardstock: unknown
Stickers: Fifties Font, Fifties Phrases, The Fifties by KFD
Light Blue, Black and Pastel Mini Brads: by KFD
Fiber: by Darice

Make a cool Fifties theme book with any number of folded pages tied into the book through two holes at the spine. Fill the pages with stories, photos and memories.

Memo of the Cool 50's

Coon-Skin Caps & Cat's-eye Glasses

Rock 'n' Roll
by Cindy Husted

Supplies
Paper: Sock Hop, Fifties Checked, Records by KFD
Cardstock: unknown
Stickers: Life Clear Quotes, Fifties Phrases, The Fifties by KFD
Fiber and Ribbon: unknown

Use Records paper to make a large pocket that appears to be filled with photos, decorative tags and text blocks.

Tip...

early newspapers

Dad never did tell us the name of this gal that he took to the school dance. It must have been a special dance...look at the dresses!

Valentines Day Dance
February 14; 8 PM - 1 AM
Formal Dress

(Opposite) Glue contrasting papers together and fold corners to overlap in the center. Cut holes for pockets, folding up edge to show contrasting paper. Attach to background paper, leaving diagonal sides as pockets.

Valentine Dance
by Jennifer Straus

Supplies
Paper: Valentine Border Red, Red Gingham, Valentine Parchment by KFD
Stickers: Valentine Cards, Valentine Punch Outs, Valentine Alphabet by KFD
Coin Envelope: by Staples
Ribbon: by JKM Ribbons

Valentine's Day
by Jennifer Straus

Supplies
Paper: Heart Stripe, Red Gingham, Valentine Parchment by KFD
Red Cardstock: unknown
Stickers: Valentine Cards, Valentine Punch Outs, Valentine Alphabet by KFD
Rickrack: by JKM Ribbons

Valentine's Day 1950
Sally ♥ James

To _____

This was our favorite tree. We played here every day. We built a treehouse, we played tag and we had the best time of our lives.

Caroll's Mom, Wilma, loved gingham, floral and polka-dot patterns. A tribute layout to her recalls Wilma's favorite red and white patterns of the '40s.

To Wilma Louise, My Mom
by Caroll Shreeve

Paper: Red Gingham, Red Flowers, Red Polka Dot, Valentine Parchment by KFD
Stickers: Valentine Alphabet, Valentine Cards by KFD
Red Mini Brads and Love Buttons: by KFD
Daisy Brad: Karen Foster Metals by KFD

The photos in the large pocket on the bottom illustrate the life story creatively folded and tucked into the large top pocket.

Tip...

Heirlooms of Tomorrow

What legacy will you leave to your children and grandchildren? The best gift you can give your descendants is a book of remembrance which includes the story of your own life.

Photograph subjects in three different poses, each zoomed-in closer than the previous. The closest shot becomes the focal point of the layout.

The Dielemans
by Wayne Dieleman

Supplies
Paper: Dusty Rose Crackle, Soft Green Crackle, Dusty Yellow Crackle by KFD
Embellishments: by Making Memories
Vellum and Cardstock: by Bazzill Basics
Heart Eyelets: by Making Memories
Rubber Stamps: Diffusion by Hampton Art
Fabric Bags (Walnut-Inked): by Moulton
Tag: by American Tag Company
Seal Image: by Club Scrap

Cut phrases from clear quotes, out of context, to create your own message.

tip...

Just Do Your Best
by Caroll Shreeve

Supplies
Paper: Light Blue Weathered Wood, Cream Weathered Wood by KFD
Stickers: Home Sweet Home, Journey Clear Quotes by KFD
Fiber: by Darice
Embellishments: Karen Foster Metals by KFD

Make a layout using two photos of your subject that are the same size and composition but with different facial expressions.

Ancestry Meets Modern

Today's Photos Are Tomorrow's Heirlooms

Combining retro papers with modern photos will turn today's layouts into tomorrow's heirlooms. Printing your photos in black-and-white or sepia tones allows you to use a variety of retro color combinations. This concept will help your ancestry book transition gently into today's layouts.

Makayla
by Debra Wilcox

Supplies
Paper: Old Book Liner, Calligraphy Collage, Shabby Map by KFD
Black Cardstock: by Bazzill Basics
Stickers: Remember, Old Tags, Old Alphabet by KFD
Wire: by Beadalon for Darice

Nikel
by Judy Ezola

Supplies
Paper: Pink Paisley,
Pink Stripe by KFD
Pale Pink Vellum:
by Bazzill Basics
Daisy Brads:
Karen Foster Metals by KFD

Trustworthy
Compassionate
Loyal
Fun
Respectful
Dedicated

Judy's simple approach to these layouts make them great examples of the adage "Less is more."

textures

Kylee
by Judy Ezola

Supplies
Paper: Purple Paisley, Purple
Stripe, Green Paisley by KFD
Stickers: Childhood Clear
Quotes by KFD
Ribbon: by Making Memories
Embellishments:
Karen Foster Metals by KFD

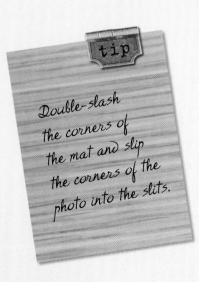

tip

Double-slash
the corners of
the mat and slip
the corners of the
photo into the slits.

In the eyes of a child

Kylee

Happy
Birthday
by Kris Silvester

Supplies
Paper: Purple Paisley,
Purple Stripe by KFD
Lilac Cardstock: by Bazzill Basics
White Vellum: by Making Memories
Brads: by Making Memories
Foam Squares: by PeelnStick
Daisy Brad: Karen Foster Metals by KFD

Just
Because
by Kris Silvester

Supplies
Paper: Pink Stripe, Pink Paisley
by KFD
Pink Cardstock: by Bazzill Basics
Computer Font: unknown
Daisy Brad: Karen Foster Metals by KFD

Congratulations!
by Kris Silvester

Supplies
Paper: Steel Blue Stripe, Steel Blue Paisley, Green
Paisley by KFD
Cardstock: by Bazzill Basics
Brad: by Making Memories
Butterfly Brad: Karen Foster Metals by KFD
Computer Font: unknown

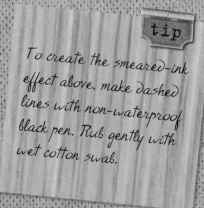

tip

To create the smeared-ink effect above, make dashed lines with non-waterproof black pen. Rub gently with wet cotton swab.

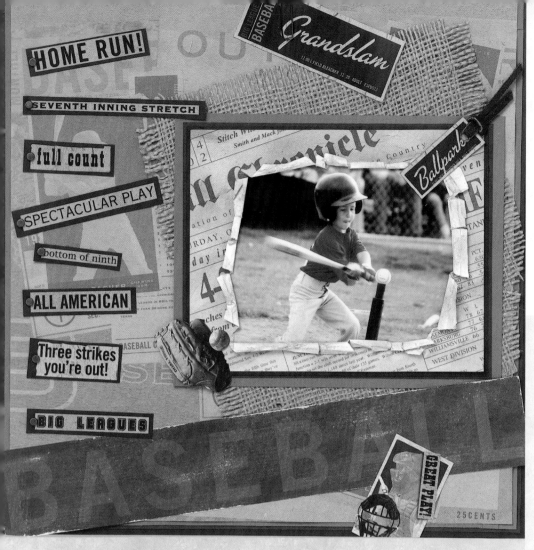

The word "baseball" was torn from Maroon Jersey paper and sanded to add texture.

Playing Ball
by Janae Lunt

Supplies
Paper: Baseball Collage, Maroon Jersey (sanded), Baseball Chronicle by KFD
Stickers: Baseball, Baseball Phrases by KFD
Cardstock: by Bazzill Basics
Antique Mini Brads: by KFD
Craft Suede Tie and Burlap

Baseball Boy
by Caroll Shreeve

Supplies
Paper: Bleachers, Baseball Chronicle by KFD
Stickers: Baseball, Varsity Alphabet, Baseball Phrases, Fathers Clear Quotes by KFD
Foam Squares: by PeelnStick
Frame: Karen Foster Metals by KFD

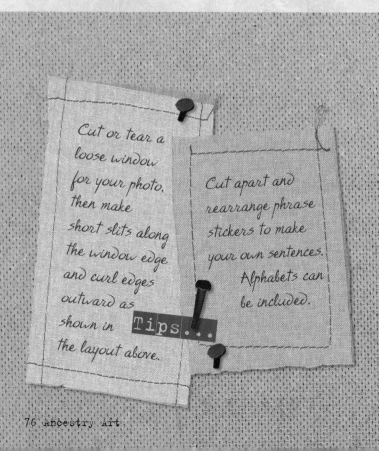

Cut or tear a loose window for your photo, then make short slits along the window edge and curl edges outward as shown in the layout above.

Cut apart and rearrange phrase stickers to make your own sentences. Alphabets can be included.

Tips...

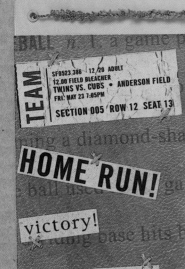

take one for the team

SF0523.386 · 12/20 ADULT
12.00 FIELD BLEACHER
TWINS VS. CUBS · ANDERSON FIELD
FRI. MAY 23 7:05PM
TEAM
SECTION 005 ROW 12 SEAT 13

HOME RUN!

victory!

BASES ARE LOADED

go the distance

Three strikes you're out!

A LEAGUE OF THEIR OWN

catcher (-er) n. 1. the player stationed behind home plate, who catches pitched balls not hit away by the batter

CLEAN UP

MINOR LEAGUE

curve, a pitch moves down and across, because of th

League of Their Own
by Kris Silvester

Supplies
Paper: Batter Up by KFD
Cardstock: by Bazzill Basics
Stickers: Baseball Definitions, Baseball, Varsity Alphabet by KFD
Eyelets: by Making Memories
Fibers: unknown

Use phrases from baseball stickers on a softball layout by choosing the words that are universal to both sports.

Cut stickers out loosely with backing in place. Position them, then pull off the backing to get them in the right spot every time!

tip...

fond memories

When taking photos, try shooting one photo zoomed in on the subject and two at a distance. Crop the distant photos smaller than the close-up. This will create balance in your layout.

It is a wise father that knows his own child
Shakespeare

Father and Son
by Janae Lunt

Supplies
Paper: Red Weathered Wood by KFD
Black, Brown and Tan Cardstock: by Bazzill Basics
Stickers: Fathers Clear Quotes by KFD
Antique Mini Brads: by KFD
Embellishments: Karen Foster Metals by KFD

Life Is Good
by Janae Lunt

Supplies
Paper: Cream Weathered
Wood by KFD
Ivory and Black Cardstock:
by Bazzill Basics
Mesh Remnant: unknown
Black Craft Cord: unknown
Metal Tags (Painted):
by Making Memories
Embellishments:
Karen Foster Metals by KFD

Weathered Wood papers are perfect for scrapbooking rustic out-of-doors photos. Tip....

love cherish

Life is good

Days gone by

memory of a noble past

... treasures of the future.

Days Gone By
by Caroll Shreeve

Supplies
Paper: Red Weathered Wood, Gold
Weathered Wood by KFD
Yellow, Orange and Green Cardstock:
by Bazzill Basics
Stickers: Heritage and Journey
Clear Quotes by KFD
Antique Mini Brads: by KFD
Paper Clip Pets: Karen Foster
Metals by KFD

**Inside of card reads: "Thank you for
giving me so many great memories."**

Make slits in your card or layout to slide

Paper Clip Pets into place.

Fishing at Daniel's Summit
by Janae Lunt

Supplies
Paper: Mustard Weathered Wood by KFD
Deep Red and Black Cardstock: by Bazzill Basics
Stickers: Old Rooster Café by KFD
Antique Mini Brads: by KFD
Jute

Fishing

We spent a long weekend at Daniel's Summit Lodge, among other things we took the fishing boat for a day on Strawberry, Takoda was excited to fish and the girls just went along for the tan. Dad caught the first fish, about 6 inches long, after that everyone was determined to catch one, Takoda then Mckenzy caught one but Allie out fished them all catching the biggest fish at a whopping 21 inches, not to bad for someone who just wants a tan. 2003

Remembrance
by Caroll Shreeve

Supplies
Paper: Cream Weathered Wood, Light Blue Weathered Wood by KFD
Cream, Dark Brown and Dark Green Cardstock: by Bazzill Basics
Stickers: Heritage and Grandmothers Clear Quotes by KFD
Fibers: by Making Memories; Darice
Oriental Coins: Karen Foster Metals by KFD

For balance, Caroll cut a small square window in her card reminiscent of the square holes in Chinese money.

Remembrance

The old trunk in the attic Is ancient and dusty

tips

Don't wait for a trip to China to use the Chinese tokens. With their loops and square holes, they can be used in many ways.

Attach Old Sign stickers to layouts so they look like they are really suspended.

never forget